Steam's Indian Summer

Steam's Indian Summer

George Heiron and Eric Treacy

London
GEORGE ALLEN & UNWIN
Boston   Sydney

First published in 1979
Reprinted 1983

GEORGE ALLEN & UNWIN LTD
40 Museum Street, London WC1A 1LU

© Colourviews Ltd, 1979

British Library Cataloguing in Publication Data

Heiron, George
   Steam's Indian summer.
   1. Locomotives – Great Britain – History –
Pictorial works
   I. Title   II. Treacy, Eric
   385'.36'10941   TJ603.4.G7   78-40561

   ISBN 0–04–385070–7

Book design by Design Matters

Typeset in 10 on 11 point Imprint by Bedford Typesetters Ltd
Printed and bound in Great Britain
by Biddles Ltd, Guildford and King's Lynn

1 (*previous page*). Giant cumulo-nimbus clouds towering in an azure sky point the way for the eastbound 'Merchant Venturer' approaching Chippenham headed by a Western Region Castle in March 1953. (GH, 1953)

Contents

2 (*following page*). The thrilling sound of a hard-working Great Western Castle echoes across the Golden Valley as a Cheltenham–Paddington express climbs the final 1 in 60 gradient to Sapperton tunnel. (GH, 1957)

Introduction

It is now just over twenty years since the appearance of the first British Railways Modernisation Plan; published during 1955, this was the first real amber light for the giants of steam. Arrangements were still in hand for the construction of further modern steam locomotives, but the last of the 'Big Four' express classes had all emerged from their respective works. It was an exciting period for the railway photographer for, even after the exchange trials of 1948, such old favourites as Stanier's Duchess and Peppercorn's A2 Pacifics, together with Swindon's Castles, had been built as reliable stand-bys for a year or two and had taken their places alongside older sisters of pre-war vintage. Later, in the 'fifties, the new British Railways Standard engines rolled off the production lines. A new generation of railway enthusiasts and railway photographers was born after World War II; they brought with them new and refreshing techniques which were made possible by new equipment and better quality films. These, added to the skills of the photographer of the 'thirties, ensured that history was well recorded.

It is almost impossible to define just how or why steam has been so evocative but from the very early days the sight, sound and even the smell of an express thundering past has attracted its tens of thousands. By the 'fifties it became obvious that the time would soon come when this still familiar form of power would be no more, though it was a shorter Indian Summer than most anticipated. Many old friends disappeared almost overnight, but such was the variety that the most avid enthusiast found it almost impossible to cover all the ground with his camera. Somewhat naturally it was to the main line that the new generation became most attracted, for who could turn away at the sight and sound of Kings and Castles, Duchesses and Jubilees, 'Flying Scotsman' or 'Clan Line'? The new rubbed shoulders with the old; the Western's Britannias with their Swindonesque names such as 'Morning Star', 'Shooting Star' and 'Mercury' ran the Cardiff expresses side by side with Castles; the London Midland's Jubilees vied with rebuilt Royal Scots; the Eastern's Britannias took over from the Sandringhams to Norwich and the Southern's West Country Pacifics replaced and ran turn by turn with those magnificent 4-4-0s of basic South Eastern and Chatham design. Others were attracted to the branch line scene, soon to pass away, and a faithful few took their cameras to the narrow gauge, but it was the gradients of Shap, Beattock, Dainton, Stoke and the Lickey which produced those thunderous exhausts as the straining, fire-eating express engines laboured their way towards the summits; the racing grounds, too, had their addicts and Little Somerford, Stoke and Bushey, which saw the magnificence of heavy trains at speed, found photographers constantly by the lineside.

The locomotive recorder had opportunities galore with the advent of colour photography. During the late 'fifties liveries changed once again and for the prestige trains some of the old colours returned almost as in the 'good old days'. For example Western Region turned out all bar its solid, slogging, freight engines in Swindon green – many lined out in gold and black – to head coaches once more resplendent in chocolate and cream, the basic coach colours reverted to LMS red and these were headed by red Pacifics on the principal London Midland Region expresses. York and Newcastle boasted shunters resplendent in North Eastern green and Liverpool Street its station pilot in Great Eastern blue.

Scotland too had its moments of glory – the one-time Great North of Scotland section kept all its locomotives spotless well into the 'fifties, glistening Stanier Black Fives double-headed trains over the Highland and West Highland lines, whilst Gresley's A4s worked out the remainder of their lives on the Glasgow to Aberdeen expresses; thus the blue livery returned once again to the Caledonian's tracks.

Not only did one try to capture the mighty express train but there was so much of the railway scene itself to record, stations still basically Victorian or Edwardian, loose coupled freight trains – the payloads of the railways – clanking their way along when the road was clear, semaphore signals, water troughs, steam sheds and marshalling yards, all needed to be recorded while the going was good. Classes

3. Pride of the London–South Wales line was the all-chocolate and cream liveried 'Red Dragon'. Here Britannia Pacific no. 70029, 'Shooting Star', restarts the westbound train from Badminton station on a wintry evening in January 1958. (GH, 1958)

which at one time seemed mundane became objects to be sought after and photographed while they were still working, and as each year's new crop of young photographers fledged themselves fresh styles appeared, bringing the scene to life in a new form. These became the days of the enthusiast specials when farewell trips were arranged for the last of a class or the closure of a branch line or later even of a one-time main line, such as the Somerset & Dorset, the Great Central and the Great Western line from Birmingham to Wolverhampton.

The enthusiast was also able to witness and record the final technical improvements made to the steam engine, the double chimney fitted to rebuilt Scots, Kings and Castles, the latter two with high degree superheat, the rebuilt Merchant Navy and West Country Pacifics, the fantastic Standard class 9Fs running at ease on heavy freights – or on express trains until the authorities thought better of it; the crowning glory of the 9F being the Swindon-built last steam engine of them all, the copper-capped chimneyed 'Evening Star'. The sad failure was the only Standard class 8 express engine 'Duke of Gloucester'.

The collapse came quickly as the diesel crept into service line by line, and by the early 'fifties the principal express trains were so hauled: a few, very few, steam locomotive classes were held in reserve. The Southern saw the last express steam engine kept hard at work until the completion of the electrification to Bournemouth in 1967; after that it was either the scrapheap or perhaps preservation.

Steam's Indian Summer occurred at the beginning of a dramatic change in the affairs of Britain's railways, it had its periods of greatness and glory but to those of us who recorded it there was the inevitable tinge of sadness at every click of the shutter – it was a race against time. As steam retreated, pressed by the alien invader into small, sometimes isolated, areas, its recorders became almost fanatical and individual locomotive rosters were sought after and treasured. The Western became the first Region to be fully dieselised, at the close of 1965; this was followed by the Southern in 1967 whilst Eastern and London Midland Regions lingered on a few more months with the final steam train – a BR-sponsored champagne special – running out of Liverpool using double-headed Black Fives and later the last Britannia Pacific, 'Oliver Cromwell'. To many eyes and in the opinion of several eminent railway engineers the slaughter was emotional rather than sensibly planned. Diesels were multiplied before being fully tried and efficient locomotives such as the class 9Fs had in some cases a working life of less than ten years.

So an age has passed but for reasons difficult to decide the emotion still lives on – even in the minds of those who were scarcely old enough to read a genuine Great Western nameplate affixed to its rightful owner. This generation and that which has known only preserved or tourist steam in Britain now take their cameras far afield to find steam in Africa, India, Indonesia or even China. In Britain and Europe the Indian Summer is over, but the sun still shines in far off places – for a while.

April 1978

GEORGE HEIRON
ERIC TREACY

Famous Headboards

Not so long ago most of the main express trains of the day had names like the 'Pembroke Coast Express', 'Tees-Tyne Pullman', 'White Rose', but now the glamour of the headboard at the top of the smoke box has gone, as have the carriage nameboards which would tell the watcher of trains the destination of the giant that thundered by. Now even the reporting numbers are disappearing, because with power signal boxes the signalman never sees a train!

4. Eastern Region A1 Pacific no. 60161, 'North British', one of the forty-nine engines of its class built to the design of A. H. Peppercorn, makes a fine sight as she leaves Edinburgh Waverley with the up 'Queen of Scots' Pullman. (ET, 1959)

5 (*left*). A muffled roar develops into a magnificent crescendo of sound as A4 Pacific no. 60028, 'Walter K. Whigham', bursts out of Hadley Wood tunnel at eighty miles per hour with the southbound 'Elizabethan'. (GH, 1954)

6 (*above*). A short stop for water at Beattock summit allows the driver of Duchess Pacific no. 46230, 'Duchess of Buccleuch', with the up 'Royal Scot' a few minutes to relax from concentration on the 'road'. (ET, 1956)

7 (*above*). Western Region 4–6–0 no. 1005, 'County of Devon', stands at the down platform of Chipping Sodbury station with a Swindon–Bristol stopping train as the westbound 'Pembroke Coast Express' roars past behind no. 7003, 'Elmley Castle'. (GH, 1955)

8 (*left*). The up 'Red Rose' passing Wavertree, Liverpool, hauled by a pre-war experimental turbo-locomotive rebuilt as a Princess Royal class. No. 46202, 'Princess Anne', heads her train for Euston. (ET, 1954)

9 The eastbound 'Red Dragon', in the charge of a shining Castle, pulls up at platform 2 at Cardiff General station.   (GH, 1958)

10 (*left*). One of the post-war Western Region 4–6–0 Castle class locomotives, no. 7006, 'Lydford Castle', takes the up 'South Wales Pullman' through Pengram yards on the outskirts of Cardiff. (GH, 1958)

11 (*right*). Princess Coronation Pacific no. 46241, 'City of Edinburgh', backs onto the Glasgow-bound 'Caledonian' at Euston on a dark and rainy day in December 1960. (GH, 1960)

12 (*below*). Glinting under the station lights at Paddington, pre-war Castle class no. 5015, 'Kingswear Castle', simmers gently at the head of platform 9 after sprinting down from Birmingham in two hours with the 'Inter-City' express. (GH, 1954)

13. British Rail Pacific no. 70024, 'Vulcan', climbs away from
Patchway tunnel with the eastbound 'Capitals United Express' shortly
after leaving Wales via the Severn tunnel.   (GH, 1958)

14. With a misty view of the Minster in the background, the down
'Flying Scotsman' passes York in the charge of A4 Pacific no. 60026,
'Miles Beevor'.   (ET, 1952)

15. With the Town Hall clock at a quarter past three, A3 Pacific no.
60046, 'Diamond Jubilee', heads the up 'White Rose Express' away from
Leeds Central Station.   (ET, 1958)

16. The eastbound 'Bristolian' takes a bend at sixty miles per hour on the way up to the Box tunnel behind 4–6–0 Castle class no. 4082, 'Windsor Castle'. Note the 'Merchant Venturer' headboard on the running board. 'Windsor Castle' probably worked that train down to Bristol in the morning.   (GH, 1949)

17 (*above*). The 'Thames-Clyde Express' heads north from Leeds City behind Britannia Pacific no. 70016, 'Ariel', watched by ex-L&Y 2–4–2T no. 50795. (ET, 1956)

18 (*right*). Driver Ted Hailstone blasts out of King's Cross with the 'Tees–Tyne Pullman' on its journey north hauled by A4 Pacific no. 60014, 'Silver Link'. This was one of the four locomotives of this class which were originally painted silver and hauled the pre-war 'Silver Jubilee'. (ET, 1948)

Famous Climbs

In the early days of railways one of the main problems of construction was to maintain, as nearly as possible, a level track-bed. Cuttings, embankments and tunnels were used, but there were times when an incline was the only means of traversing the planned route. Of those inclines the steepest of any length was the Lickey, just north of Bromsgrove on what was the Birmingham and Gloucester Railway, with a grade of 1 in 37.5. Steam engines had to work extra hard on the steeper grades, and the display of smoke and steam they produced made the inclines favourite places for the railway photographer.

19 (*left*). The thunder of twin exhausts suddenly shatters the stillness of late autumn as the southbound 'Pines Express' emerges from Devonshire tunnel on the long climb from Bath to Combe Down tunnel. (GH, 1953)

20 (*above*). A wartime photograph of grimy streamlined Princess Coronation class Pacific LMS no. 6223, 'Princess Alice', seen approaching Shap summit with a Euston–Glasgow train. The streamlining was removed shortly after the war. (ET, 1942)

21 (*left*). Ex-LMS class 2 4–4–0 no. 40657 pilots a rebuilt Royal Scot over Shap summit with a Glasgow–Manchester train. (ET, 1949)

22 (*top*). The sharp explosive blast from the chimney of Castle class locomotive no. 5018, 'St Mawes Castle', reaches a deafening climax as she passes Frampton Crossing signal box on the way up to Sapperton tunnel with a twelve-coach Cheltenham–Paddington express. (GH, 1955)

23 (*right*). A down Perth–Euston express passing Great Strickland, between Penrith and Shap summit, hauled by Princess Coronation class 4–6–2 no. 46238, 'City of Carlisle'. (ET, 1955)

24 (*above*). The northbound 'Pines Express'
roars up the Mangotsfield cut-off, between Bath
and Yate, in sub-zero temperatures. (GH, 1952)

25 (*right*). Western Region Castle class 4–6–0
no. 5040, 'Stokesay Castle', takes the 1 in 60
bank to Sapperton tunnel with the up
'Cheltenham Spa Express'. (GH, 1955)

26. Two British Railways Standard 4–6–0s, a class 5 piloted by class 4 no. 75023, march in tandem up Devonshire bank out of Bath with the southbound 'Pines Express'. (GH, 1962)

27. Modified Great Western Hall class no. 6961, 'Stedham Hall', takes
a bend at speed above Brimscombe, on the way up to Sapperton tunnel
with a heavy Cheltenham–Paddington express.   (GH, 1955)

28 (*above*). A fourteen-coach train was hard work for any steam locomotive on Beattock, as this Princess Coronation Pacific finds out at the head of the down 'Royal Scot'. (GH, 1954)

29 (*below*). The down 'Royal Scot' makes Princess Coronation no. 46222, 'Queen Mary', work hard as they pass Harthope on the way to Beattock summit. (ET, 1958)

30 (*right*). A Great Western-built Hall class 4–6–0 no. 6905, 'Cloughton Hall', pounds up the winding 1 in 60 to Sapperton tunnel on a cold but sunny day in January 1955. (GH, 1955)

31. A Brimscombe-based 2–6–2 tank pushes hard
while banking a Gloucester–Swindon freight
on the 1 in 60 grade above Chalford.
(GH, 1955)

32. The typical throaty sound of the Midland exhaust of 4–4–0 class 2 no. 40563 blends with the 'shuffling sandpaper' sound of the Bulleid West Country Pacific no. 34044, 'Woolacombe', as the two heave the thirteen-coach 'Pines Express' up Devonshire bank on their way south out of Bath. (GH, 1954)

33 (*above*). Western Region Castle class no. 7035, 'Ogmore Castle', pilots another Castle up the 1 in 60 incline to Sapperton tunnel with an up Carmarthen–Paddington express which had been diverted via Gloucester and Stroud because of engineering work in the Severn tunnel. (GH, 1954)

34 (*right*). The crisp exhaust from the straining Great Western 2–8–0 echoes in the cutting and drowns the lonely singing of the telegraph wires as she slowly moves an eastbound freight up to Sapperton tunnel. (GH, 1955)

35. One of the hazards of moving a heavy train out of Euston is Camden
bank. Here Princess Coronation Pacific no. 46248, 'City of Leeds',
works hard to gather speed with a heavy express bound for Holyhead.
(ET, 1962)

36. No. 46232, 'Duchess of Montrose', at the head of a Glasgow--Birmingham express in full cry as they pass Chigton on Shap. (ET, 1958)

Station Scenes

The railway station was always a favourite place for those who wanted to watch steam trains and in particular the larger stations and junctions where traffic was heaviest. In addition to there being plenty to see there was the great advantage of means of access – you could even go there by train! There was shelter if the weather became inclement and on the larger stations the comfort of a refreshment room and at one time even a fire. At termini, even those only mildly interested in trains would go to the platform end to see 'what we are going to have on'. But most of all stations were good places to get near to the engines and to be able to take time getting the pictures you wanted.

37. Britannia Pacific no. 70052, 'Firth of Tay', easing a heavily loaded Glasgow–Manchester train on its way south out of Carlisle Citadel. (ET, 1955)

38 (*left*). Unrebuilt West Country Pacific no. 34002, 'Salisbury', in immaculate condition, stands in Ilfracombe station in May 1961, while her crew watch the camera. (GH, 1961)

39 (*inset left*). Driver Eames and Fireman Rainbow have just brought a Wolverhampton–Paignton holiday extra into Bristol and are waiting for the signal to move off to the sheds. A fresh engine will take their train on to Paignton. (GH, 1961)

40. The down 'Flying Scotsman' makes the most of a brief stop at Newcastle Central to take on water. A4 Pacific no. 60024, 'Kingfisher', sounds her chime whistle as she is about to start. (ET, 1958)

41. Reminiscent of a battleship sliding into port, unrebuilt Bulleid
Merchant Navy Pacific no. 35019, 'French Line CGT' glides into
Salisbury station with a Bournemouth-bound express.   (GH, 1956)

42. With the castle standing proudly in the background, Silver Jubilee class no. 45689, 'Ajax', leaves Lancaster with a Barrow-in-Furness–Euston train. (ET, 1948)

43 (*above*). Princess Coronation class Pacific no. 46248, 'City of Leeds', in blue livery, moves the fully loaded fifteen-coach 'Mid-day Scot' out of Euston Station, bound for Glasgow. (GH, 1955)

44 (*right*). Journey's end: ex-LNER A1 Pacific no. 60140, 'Balmoral', stands at King's Cross after bringing in an express from Edinburgh Waverley. (GH, 1955)

45 (*above*). Silver Jubilee 4–6–0 no. 45685, 'Barfleur', leaving York with a Newcastle–Bristol train. (ET, 1956)

46 (*left*). Great Western King no. 6007, 'King William III', recently outshopped, waits in the middle road at Bath Spa on a running-in turn to Swindon. (GH, 1953)

47 (*right*). The elegance of Bath is enhanced by the graceful curve of the railway and the thirteen-coach Plymouth–Paddington express standing in Spa station.   (GH, 1953)

48 (*right*). A Bradford-Bristol train passes a foxglove-decorated platform as it leaves Derby hauled by Silver Jubilee no. 45626, 'Seychelles'.
(ET, 1954)

49 (*below*). With sand being forced under the driving wheels, rebuilt Bulleid Pacific no. 35030, 'Elder Dempster Lines', moves a Southampton and Bournemouth express out of Waterloo.
(GH, 1958)

50. Southern Region unrebuilt Merchant Navy
Pacific no. 35009, 'Shaw Savill', restarts the
Waterloo-bound 'Atlantic Coast Express' from
Salisbury.   (GH, 1956)

51 (*left*). The down 'Royal Scot' eases gently under the road bridge at the north end of Carlisle Citadel station with Princess Coronation Pacific no. 46230, 'Duchess of Buccleuch', at the head. (ET, 1954)

52 (*bottom of page*). Pollution at Carlisle: Princess Coronation Pacific no. 46221, 'Queen Elizabeth', puts up a good plume of curly black smoke as she waits to leave Citadel station with a Birmingham Scotsman. (ET, 1952)

53 (*right*). A Carlisle–Edinburgh train via the Waverley route, with A2 Pacific no. 60535, 'Hornet's Beauty', makes a stately exit from Carlisle Citadel. (ET, 1951)

54 (*left*). Ex-LMS Silver Jubilee no. 45662, 'Kempenfelt', stands at platform 9, Bristol Temple Meads, with a northbound 'Devonian'. (GH, 1955)

55 (*below*). The driver watches for the green light from the cab window of his rebuilt Bulleid Pacific, ready to move out of Waterloo with the 'Atlantic Coast Express' bound for Exeter and Ilfracombe. (GH, 1957)

56. With the driver talking to the guard and the fireman to an inspector,
A4 Pacific no. 60009, 'Union of South Africa', waits at Edinburgh
Waverley at the head of the 'Elizabethan'. (ET, 1955)

57 (*above*). A feather of steam from the chimney, the fireman tending the lamps, and in a few minutes no. 6001, 'King Edward VII', will be leaving Paddington with an evening express to Plymouth. (GH, 1954)

58 (*left*). Platform 8 at Paddington, a busy scene as Britannia Pacific no. 70020, 'Mercury', arrives with an early morning express from Bristol. (GH, 1954)

59 (*right*). Brewing up and waiting their turns at Carlisle Citadel, Silver Jubilee no. 45724, 'Warspite', and Princess Royal Pacific no. 46201, 'Princess Elizabeth', one of the first two engines of this class which were built in 1933. (ET, 1958)

60 (*left*). Heading through the gardens by Princes Street, Edinburgh, A3 Pacific no. 60099, 'Call Boy', pulls a Dundee express out of Waverley station.   (GH, 1950)

61 (*above*). Immaculate rebuilt West Country class Pacific no. 34100, 'Appledore', pulls out of Victoria station with the 'Golden Arrow' – pride of the Southern Region.   (GH, 1960)

62 (*left*). A peaceful bird's-eye scene from the wooded hills of the Slade Valley as an unrebuilt Bulleid West Country Pacific moves a three-coach train out of Ilfracombe station.   (GH, 1961)

63 (*right*). The arrival platforms at King's Cross station in the early 1950s with A3 Pacific no. 60103, 'Flying Scotsman', in her last days of service with British Rail before preservation. (GH, 1955)

64 (*below*). Rebuilt Bulleid Pacific no. 34100, 'Appledore', at Victoria station before the departure of the 'Golden Arrow'.   (GH, 1961)

65 (*upper left*). Manchester, London Road: an up express for Euston pulls steadily away with Britannia Pacific no. 70032, 'Tennyson'. (ET, 1958)

66 (*lower left*). The up 'Merseyside Express' with Princess Royal class no. 46208, 'Princess Helena Victoria', at its head at Picton Road, Liverpool. (ET, 1958)

67. With sand on the track and an echoing exhaust, Princess Coronation class Pacific no. 46248, 'City of Leeds', starts the 'Mid-day Scot' out of Euston on a dull August day in 1953. (GH, 1953)

68. Waterloo departure platforms with the old wooden awnings. Rebuilt West Country Pacific no. 34037, 'Clovelly', on the left, and rebuilt Merchant Navy no. 35025, 'Brocklebank Line', backing onto a West of England express. (GH, 1962)

69 (*right*). With the North British Hotel clock standing at 11.05, a King's Cross-bound express pulls out of Edinburgh Waverley behind A3 Pacific no. 60094, 'Colorado'.   (ET, 1953)

70 (*below*). On a damp day two ex-LNER 4–6–0s wait at the head of their trains at King's Cross suburban platforms. On the left is a B1 no. 61331 and on the right B17/6, 'Aske Hall'. (GH, 1955)

71 (*below*). A handsome rebuilt Royal Scot no. 46105, 'Cameron Highlander', at platform 2, Glasgow Central. (GH, 1954)

72 (*right*). Another rebuilt Royal Scot class 4–6–0 no. 46106, 'Gordon Highlander', waits at Euston with a good head of steam as she starts the 'Red Rose' on her way north. (GH, 1955)

73 (*left*). 'Neil Gow' – A3 Pacific no. 60082 – leaving York with a Newcastle–Liverpool train while two freight trains wait for 'Neil Gow' and her train to clear the crossovers. (ET, 1958)

74 (*right*). People hurry eagerly to the platform end at Cardiff to get a close-up view of Britannia Pacific no. 70018, 'Flying Dutchman', at the head of the all-chocolate and cream liveried 'Red Dragon' waiting to depart for Paddington. (GH, 1951)

75 (*below*). The minute hand jumps to fifteen minutes past eleven and the whistle blows for the departure of the 'Merchant Venturer' from platform 1 at Paddington with a King in charge. (GH, 1952)

76 (*above*). A running-in turn for A1 Pacific no. 60146, 'Peregrine', waiting at Leeds Central station with a morning train for East Anglia. (ET, 1959)

77 (*left*). Silver Jubilee class 4–6–0 no. 45694, 'Bellerophon', leaving Leeds City at the head of the 'Waverley'. (ET, 1960)

78 (*right*). After bringing an early morning express down from Glasgow, Princess Royal class Pacific no. 46208, 'Princess Helena Victoria', backs her empty train out of Euston. (GH, 1953)

79. Just arrived from Southampton, rebuilt
West Country Pacific no. 34100, 'Appledore',
has come to rest at Waterloo. (GH, 1960)

Passenger Trains

It was the steam-hauled passenger train above all that created the elegance and sense of speed which more modern forms of traction seem to lack, even though they may actually be faster. Gone is the trail of white smoke and steam, the echoing screech of a steam whistle and the glinting of sunshine on glistening paint and the bright steel of the rapidly moving connecting rods and valve gear. Also gone is the friendly wave of the driver or fireman to a lineside watcher or photographer. Somehow diesels and electrics, though efficient, seem so inanimate.

80. Eastern Region B12 class 4–6–0 no. 61541 leaving Grantham station with a three-coach local train for Nottingham. (ET, 1949)

81 (*left*). The low sunshine lights up Princess Royal Pacific no. 46203, 'Princess Margaret Rose', as she moves her Birmingham–Glasgow train past Kingmoor, Carlisle.   (ET, 1962)

82 (*below*). A Western Region Hall class 4–6–0 passing St Mary's Crossing signal box with a Cheltenham–Paddington special.   (GH, 1956)

83. A British Railways class 5 and a Stanier Black Five double-head the afternoon Mallaig–Fort William–Glasgow express, which carries through sleeping cars for King's Cross, up the gradient past Monessie Gorge between Roy Bridge and Rannoch Moor in March 1961. (GH, 1961)

84. Evening sunlight reflects on the wet track as an eastbound 'Pembroke Coast Express' takes water at speed from Chipping Sodbury troughs. (GH, 1959)

85. On a hazy September evening in 1960, Silver Jubilee no. 45651, 'Shovell', roars through Westerleigh yards past Westerleigh North signal box with a Bristol–Bradford express. (GH, 1960)

86 (*above*). An evening Cardiff–Paddington express breasts the summit through Badminton station at the end of the eleven-mile 1 in 300 climb from Stoke Gifford. (GH, 1955)

87 (*left*). British Railways Standard 4–6–2 class 7MT no. 70025, 'Western Star', speeding towards Paddington near Hullavington (between Badminton and Little Somerford), one of the fastest stretches on the Bristol–London main line. (GH, 1951)

88 (*above*). The 1.35 pm Bristol–London Sundays only express leaving Alderton tunnel, east of Badminton, on the descending bank to Little Somerford. (GH, 1952)

89 (*left*). Princess Royal Pacific no. 46206, 'Princess Marie Louise', passing Thrimby with a Glasgow–Birmingham train. (ET, 1955)

90 (*below*). Great cumulo-nimbus tower over London as the westbound 'Atlantic Coast Express' sweeps through Clapham Junction with a handsome rebuilt Merchant Navy Pacific at the head. (GH, 1961)

91 (*right*). Southern Region unrebuilt Bulleid West Country Pacific no. 34006, 'Bude', climbs through the rocks and ferns of the beautiful Slade Valley to Mortehoe with the Ilfracombe portion of the 'Atlantic Coast Express'. (GH, 1961)

92 (*left*). In the pleasant days of gas lamps and quiet country lanes the Ilfracombe section of the up 'Atlantic Coast Express' climbs away through the hills to Mortehoe and Barnstaple. (GH, 1961)

93 (*below*). A truly rural scene. The Stroud–Chalford stopping train near St Mary's Crossing Halt, with Great Western 1400 class 0–4–2T no. 1424 in August 1953. (GH, 1953)

94. The lonely upper reaches of the Golden Valley are bathed in evening sunlight as no. 7926, 'Willey Hall', rolls downhill from the tunnel with a Swindon–Gloucester stopping train in August 1952.   (GH, 1952)

95. The tranquillity of the River Avon at Saltford
near Bath is disturbed by a Bristol–Paddington
express. (GH, 1953)

96 (*above*). A down Waverley express passing Dent station on the old Midland Railway's Settle–Carlisle line, hauled by Silver Jubilee class 4–6–0 no. 45675, 'Hardy'. (ET, 1958)

97 (*right*). Western Region Castle class 4–6–0 no. 7024, 'Powis Castle', nearing Little Somerford at 100 mph at the end of the run down from Badminton with the 11.45 am Bristol–Paddington non-stop. (GH, 1954)

98 (*above*). A springtime scene in woods at Thrimby with a Glasgow–Birmingham train hurrying by, hauled by Princess Royal Pacific no. 46210, 'Lady Patricia'. (ET, 1961)

99 (*left*). Britannia Pacific no. 70029, 'Shooting Star', gathers speed through the busy Pengam Yards, Cardiff, with a Carmarthen–Paddington express. (GH, 1954)

100. A down Newcastle express between the tunnels at King's Cross headed by the record-breaking Gresley A4 Pacific no. 60022, 'Mallard', while in the background no. 60010, 'Dominion of Canada', gently runs down the slope from King's Cross locomotive shed.   (ET, 1954)

101 (*above*). A Caprotti-valved British Railways class 9 2–10–0 eases up to Westerleigh Junction before negotiating the sharp curve down to the Midland main line with a Plymouth–Manchester express. (GH, 1960)

102 (*right*). Platform 12, Bristol Temple Meads station. The time is approaching 7.20 pm, when Silver Jubilee 4–6–0 no. 45619, 'Nigeria', will move out into the rain and head north with the Royal Mail and sleeper express for Birmingham, York and Newcastle. (GH, 1956)

Trains at Night

There was something almost frightening about a steam-hauled express train dashing through a country station at night with whistle screeching and lights flashing from the carriage windows. It is beyond the technical means of photography to record this for us, but a train in a station at night was an awe-inspiring sight that cannot be matched with our more modern methods of traction. The platform lighting gave a contrast that added power to the scene, and the steam blowing off from the safety-valves, being whiter in the lower temperature, caught the light and was dramatized by the dark background of the sky or station roof.

On the signal gantry: MEMBERS OF THE PUBLIC MUST NOT PASS BEYOND THIS NOTICE

103 (*above*). Class A3 Gresley Pacific no. 60046, 'Diamond Jubilee', at the head of the overnight express for Edinburgh, waits for the right-away from King's Cross. In a few minutes the heavy sleeping-cars will be swinging out past the colour-light signals and gathering speed northwards through the night, into the dawn of a Saturday morning in Scotland.   (GH, 1955)

104 (*left*). The sharp bark of exhaust punctuates the roar of escaping steam, as with a brief slip of driving wheels on the damp rails no. 5007, 'Rougemont Castle', restarts the down 'Red Dragon' out of Badminton station.   (GH, 1954)

105. Eastern Region A1 Peppercorn Pacific no.
60124, 'Kenilworth', awaits the right-away at
King's Cross with the 'Night Scotsman'.
(GH, 1959)

106 (*above*). Rebuilt Battle of Britain Pacific
no. 34060, '25 Squadron', takes water at
Salisbury while at the head of an evening
express to Waterloo, and gives the driver an
opportunity to get busy with the oilcan.
(GH, 1962)

107 (*right*). The roar of safety valves fills the
night air and the ground vibrates to the rumble
of boiler pressure as rebuilt Merchant Navy
Pacific no. 35010, 'Blue Star', prepares to restart
an evening Waterloo–Exeter express from
Salisbury station in December 1961.
(GH, 1961)

108. Time for a smoke and a chat at Westerleigh yards as an LMS
Patriot class 4–6–0 no. 45519, 'Lady Godiva', awaits the 'line clear' with
a heavy freight bound for Scotland.   (GH, 1960)

109 (*above*). British Rail's massive class 9 2–10–0 no. 92118 brings her Birmingham–Bristol freight to a halt at Westerleigh West junction to allow a South Wales–Paddington express through on the up main line. (GH, 1962)

110 (*inset above*). The fire is glowing brightly from the cab of British Rail Standard class 5MT 4–6–0 no. 73003 as she pulls up beside the signal box at the south end of Mangotsfield station with a Newcastle–Bristol express.   (GH, 1962)

111 (*left*). LMS Black Five 4–6–0 no. 44855 stands at platform 5 in Bristol Temple Meads station on a misty December evening. (GH, 1953)

112 (*above*). Looking like prehistoric monsters from the mists of time, two A4 Pacifics, no. 60034, 'Lord Faringdon', and no. 60022, 'Mallard', pull up in the arrival platforms at King's Cross. (GH, 1955)

Bridges and Tunnels

Of the many facets of railway construction it was the bridges and tunnel entrances that gave most scope for the imagination of the railway builders. All had their distinctive styles, and there was no mistaking a Great Western tunnel entrance for one on the Midland or the Great Northern. These variations in styles of architecture add variety to pictures of trains. It was always an exciting moment when you first heard the rumble coming from a tunnel entrance and the expectation of the moment when the train burst out into the daylight and you were able to see what class of engine was at the head.

113 (*left*). A busy scene between the tunnels outside Newport station in the days of pannier tanks, prairie tanks and carriage destination boards. (GH, 1956)

114 (*above*). On one of the most scenic routes in Great Britain. A southbound Mallaig–Fort William–Glasgow, Queen Street express with through sleepers for King's Cross rumbles over a bridge on Rannock Moor south of Spean Bridge. (GH, 1961)

115 (*left*). A down freight train headed by K3/2 2–6–0 no. 61983 crossing Stephenson's Border Bridge at Berwick-upon-Tweed. (ET, 1962)

116 (*above*). Silver Jubilee 4–6–0 no. 45562, 'Alberta', leaving Wickwar tunnel with the northbound 'Devonian'. (GH, 1954)

117 (*above*). Britannia Pacific no. 70020,
'Mercury', emerges from Tiverton tunnel, west of
Bath, with the down 'Merchant Venturer'.
(GH, 1951)

118 (*right*). Thunderheads boil high in the
summer sky as Silver Jubilee 4–6–0 no. 45564,
'New South Wales', roars under the GWR
viaduct at Westerleigh with an afternoon Bristol–
York express.   (GH, 1954)

119. A Sunday Bristol–Paddington express hauled by no. 7022, 'Hereford Castle', threads Box Middle Hill tunnel on the way up to Box tunnel.   (GH, 1951)

120. A Bristol–Paddington express about to enter
the western portals of Brunel's Box tunnel.
(GH, 1951)

121 (*left*). The thunderous exhaust beats of ex-GWR no. 5040, 'Stokesay Castle', are magnified by the confines of the deep cutting as she enters Sapperton tunnel with the London-bound 'Cheltenham Spa Express'. (GH, 1955)

122 (*bottom of page*). In a fog of smoke, steam, and brake-shoe dust, no. 5042, 'Winchester Castle', emerges from Sapperton tunnel and starts the steep descent to Stroud with a Paddington–Cheltenham express. (GH, 1955)

123 (*right*). Unrebuilt Battle of Britain Pacific no. 34086, '219 Squadron', emerges from the picturesque portals of Ilfracombe tunnel, in the hills above the resort, with a stopping train from Exeter. (GH, 1960)

Freight Trains

It was the freight train that really opened one's eyes to the vast power of steam – small coupled wheels to give greater tractive effort, often straining at every revolution, and a train of seventy or eighty wagons disappearing into the distance. The pace was slow and with the engine working hard the exhaust steam and smoke often went high into the air in a great column and did not hug the train as was the case with the expresses. Then at the end of the train came the brake-van, with a curl of smoke from the chimney on cold days.

124. British Rail class 9 2–10–0 no. 92135 moves slowly up to the starting signal at Westerleigh yards before joining the main line with a northbound freight. (GH, 1961)

125 (*left*). Western Region modified Hall class 4–6–0 no. 7912, 'Little Linford Hall', heaves a long freight up the incline to Westerleigh junction, bound for Bristol. (GH, 1959)

126 (*below*). An LMS Fowler class 4 0–6–0 no. 44558 smokes up Standish Junction signal box as it trundles past with a long string of empty wagons for Gloucester. (GH, 1956)

127 (*above*). LNER K3 class 2–6–0 no. 61838 leaves York avoiding line with a train of ash. (ET, 1963)

128 (*right*). A southbound freight train hauled by class 5 4–6–0 no. 44755, seen just north of Hawes Junction on the Settle–Carlisle line. (ET, 1958)

129 (*above*). A GWR
28 class 2–8–0 no. 3845
hammers under the
road bridge at the west
end of Badminton
station with a coal
train from South
Wales. (GH, 1953)

130 (*left*). A Stanier
class 8 2–8–0 no. 48220
takes southbound
tonnage through the
picturesque Yate
station. (GH, 1960)

131. British Railways class 9 2–10–0 gallops
westward through Coalpit Heath with a train of
Esso tankers bound for South Wales in November
1962.   (GH, 1962)

132 (*left*). A GWR 28 class 2–8–0 no. 3845 climbs steadily up the 1 in 60 gradient to Sapperton tunnel with a heavy coal train. (GH, 1961)

133 (*below*). A Welsh coal train assisted at the rear by a 2–6–2T from Brimscombe shed heads towards Sapperton tunnel. (GH, 1961)

134. A class 9 2–10–0 no. 92227 heads its
northbound freight under the arches after leaving
Westerleigh.   (GH, 1962)

Shed Scenes

Visiting a shed was always an occasion – usually preceded by some weeks of negotiations with the railway company or region for a 'shed permit'. This entailed an indemnity form, signed over a plum-coloured 6d stamp, which meant if you fell under an engine or down an ashpit it was your fault. Once you arrived 'on' the shed you were truly amongst the giants and it was up to you to persuade the drivers to move their engines to a place where you thought you could get the best picture. The drivers always appreciated any prints of photographs you took of their engines.

135 (*left*). The setting sun glints on the slide bars of a Black Five 4–6–0 as she gets attention from the driver at Westerleigh yards. (GH, 1958)

136 (*top*). Dumfries Motive Power Depot in the early 1950s. The locomotives identifiable are Black Five 4–6–0 no. 44884, LMS class 2 4–4–0 no. 40576, Black Five no. 45480, and ex-Caledonian Railway 2F 0–6–0 no. 57405. (GH, 1956)

137 (*above*). Silver Jubilee class 4–6–0 no. 45681, 'Aboukir' and rebuilt Royal Scot no. 46159, 'The Royal Air Force' stand together outside the sheds at Edge Hill. (ET, 1955)

138. Princess Coronation Pacific no. 46250, 'City of Lichfield', on the turntable at Carlisle, Upperby. (ET, 1963)

139. Rebuilt Royal Scot no. 46127, 'Old Contemptibles', receives attention from a lone cleaner at Holyhead. (ET, 1948)

140 (*right*). In the early morning mist the driver climbs aboard Britannia class 4–6–2 no. 70026, 'Polar Star', at Canton sheds, Cardiff. (GH, 1956)

141 (*above*). Great Western King class 4–6–0 no. 6012, 'King Edward VI', gleams in the low December sunshine at Bristol, Bath Road shed, as she is readied for the high-speed, non-stop sprint to London with the 'Bristolian'. (GH, 1954)

142. A row of Hall class 4–6–0s are ready for
duty outside the sheds at Canton, Cardiff.
The two nearest the camera are modified Hall no.
6994, 'Baggrave Hall', and standard Hall no.
5918, 'Walton Hall'.   (GH, 1956)

143. Eastern Region A4 Pacific preserved and repainted as LNER no. 4498, 'Sir Nigel Gresley', in the shed at Upperby, Carlisle.   (ET, 1968)

144. A busy scene at Cardiff Canton sheds with a mixture of GWR and British Rail Standard locomotives. (GH, 1956)

145 (*left*). Barrow Road, Bristol, LMS shed with five classes of locomotive to be seen: two Black Fives, a Silver Jubilee, a GWR pannier tank, a BR class 9 2–10–0, and a Fowler 0–6–0. The Bristol–Birmingham main lines are in the background. (GH, 1961)

146 (*above*). Sunday morning in the engine roundhouse at Swindon, and Castle class 4–6–0 no. 5045, 'Earl of Dudley', takes a well-earned rest under the smoke duct. (GH, 1955)

147. Looking as majestic as an ocean liner, ex-GWR 4–6–0 no. 6013, 'King Henry VIII', stands outside the locomotive construction shops at Swindon after a major overhaul and repaint. (GH, 1955)

Index

NB. The references are to photograph numbers and *not* to page numbers.